# My First Adventures

# MY FIRST TRIP TO THE
# AQUARIUM

By Katie Kawa

Gareth Stevens
Publishing

Please visit our website, www.garethstevens.com. For a free color catalog of all our high-quality books, call toll free 1-800-542-2595 or fax 1-877-542-2596.

**Library of Congress Cataloging-in-Publication Data**

Kawa, Katie.
My first trip to the aquarium / Katie Kawa.
     p. cm. — (My first adventures)
Includes index.
ISBN 978-1-4339-7301-7 (pbk.)
ISBN 978-1-4339-7302-4 (6-pack)
ISBN 978-1-4339-7300-0 (library binding)
1. Public aquariums—Juvenile literature. 2. Aquatic biology—Juvenile literature. I. Title.
QL78.K39 2012
597.073—dc23
                                    2011043598

First Edition

Published in 2013 by
**Gareth Stevens Publishing**
111 East 14th Street, Suite 349
New York, NY 10003

Copyright © 2013 Gareth Stevens Publishing

Editor: Katie Kawa
Designer: Andrea Davison-Bartolotta

All Illustrations by Planman Technologies

Printed in the United States of America

CPSIA compliance information: Batch #CS12GS: For further information contact Gareth Stevens, New York, New York at 1-800-542-2595.

# Contents

Today I am going to
a place with lots of fish.
It is called the aquarium.

AQUARIUM

5

First, my dad
gets a map.
This shows us where
all of the fish are.

The fish live
in big tanks.

Other animals live there too. I like the turtles.

My mom likes
the dolphins.

13

A man teaches them tricks. He is a trainer.

15

I go to the touch tank.
A worker helps me
touch the animals.

I touch a blue crab.
It is big!

It has 10 legs.

21

I learned a lot
about fish today!

# Words to Know

crab

dolphin

tank

# Index

24